ISBN - 978-1939484338

Copyright © 2010, 201⁵

Second Edition

Katmoran Publications
225 Main Street
Bolton, MA
United States of America
www.katmoranpublications.com

ACKNOWLEDGEMENTS

I would like to thank all my friends who supported and encouraged me during my work on this book. Thank you to my family for your great support. Special thanks to my dear friend and fellow award-winning author & poet Marta Moran Bishop.

Thank you always to my friend Cor van der Kamp for reading and commenting on the early versions of Charm.

Thank you to my publisher Katmoran Publications. Thank you also to my editor Jill K. Sayre.

FOREWORD

This book is a gripping account of a remarkable experience in my life. It is a story that tells how things are hard to acquire and easy to lose when even slightly neglected. It is a story that makes the reader think about the existence of a higher power and the other world. It is a story that shows anyone can be entrusted with a certain mission from above. Or simply, it is a story about a miracle. Sometimes miracles happen in our lives.

This is the true story of Charm.

Praise for Charm: An Amazing Story of a Little Black Cat.

"Children and adults will laugh and cry through the experience of reading this brief, heartfelt book about the miracle of Charm."
– Midwest Book Review.

"A beautifully illustrated, real-life story of rescue, love, loss and rebirth. Charm is very honest account of the life of a little black cat. Full of emotion, Charm is the perfect book for anyone who has a lost or terminal pet, and a great way to start a discussion with your child. Well done, Leyla."
– Hayley Rose.

"A delightful little story with depth of meaning inside it. Being a Religion teacher who is currently teaching a small unit on miracles, this book came to me at exactly the right time. Although some people may consider the events in this book to be coincidences, Leyla certainly shows how they can feel like miracles from God."
- Chris Miles.

"What a great book! Leyla touched on all the emotions and showed how important the relationship is between humans and their animals, and humans with other humans. A wonderful read and a labor of love. Well done, Leyla!"

– **Gary R**.

"This well written story would be excellent to help teach children about the responsibilities involved in owning and caring for a pet. It would also be a great book to help children who are mourning the loss of their own pet."

– **Harley.**

"Wonderful little book of an uncanny tale. Leyla Atke shares a true story that you can tell she is compelled to tell because it is so filled with charm and magic. After reading this lovingly written book with its fanciful illustrations, I couldn't get the story out of my head. The extraordinary other-worldliness of it made me wonder and reflect what is life and what of it do we know. You'll like this book and will be compelled to share the story yourself! Nice."

– **Ace.**

"Leyla illustrates her book well, with both photographs and illustrations, writes a story that has wonderful overtones of the spiritual world about which we know so little, and in her own way, introduces the reader to the realm of afterlife and the reincarnation of beloved animals. And she makes it work on every level. And by story's end, we KNOW this is a memoir!"

– Grady Harp.

"Leyla Atke's book "Charm: An Amazing Story of a Little Black Cat" is a little book with great magic and heart. It is a book that I don't believe you have to be a cat lover for it to touch your heart, instead if you are a lover of life, you will find this book worth the time to read.

It drew me in from page one and held my interest sometimes in sorrow, when tears sprang from my eyes unbidden, and sometimes in delight for the little black cat held enchantment in its soul.

Ms. Atke held me in the palm of her hand as she laid out her story. It left me believing in the value of hope and miracles and wishing it wouldn't end. I believe Ms. Atke has a definite talent for story telling than can only continue to grow. She weaves her tale so naturally; she makes you believe it is all true and if it isn't, it should be.

The book contains charming illustrations by the author and could be read by and to children as well as enjoyed by an adult."

– Marta Moran Bishop – Author & Poet.

Winner of these prestigious INTERNATIONAL literary awards:

2015 - Readers Favorite Honorable Mention
(Non-Fiction Animals)

2014 - Readers Favorite Honorable Mention
(Non-Fiction Short Story)

2012 - International Book Awards Finalist
(Children's Non-Fiction)

2012 - Readers Favorite Finalist
(Non-Fiction Animals)

CHARM

AN AMAZING STORY OF
A LITTLE BLACK CAT

Written and Illustrated by

Leyla Atke

TABLE OF CONTENTS

CHAPTER 1

I was inspired to write this book by an amazing and strange experience I had a few years back.

It was a hot summer day in June 2006 and I was leaving work for a break. I was heading to the beauty parlor that was not too far away, to get a new hairstyle. Because the parlor was at the end of the park, I had to hurry. But first, I needed to cross a couple of two-way roads.

The traffic was quite heavy as it was the usual break time for all the offices. Luckily, I had phoned ahead to make the appointment, so they were waiting for me.

At a big intersection near the roundabout, I noticed from afar something small and black moving among the rushing cars. I decided to walk closer and see what it was.

At first, I thought it was a cat that had been run over by a car.

When I got closer, I saw a little black kitten sitting in the middle of the road, which was momentarily free of cars. However, traffic would soon resume and the kitten would be crushed, and only a dark spot would have remained on the asphalt.

Surprisingly, there was nobody around other than me, the cars, and the kitten. At that moment, on both sides of the intersection, the cars were waiting for the green light. This gave me the chance to cross both roads and get to the kitten, drivers watching with curiosity on the empty traffic way.

I was surprised to find that the kitten was not hurt. I wondered how it got to the middle of the intersection without being crushed at the roadside. I gently grabbed it and crossed another street before reaching the park.

The kitten looked very scared, but didn't try to jump out of my hands. The little one looked at me all the time. Gradually, the kitten calmed down as I held it in my hands, and began to feel more comfortable.

It's like it fell from the sky, I thought in amazement. Or someone might have thrown the kitten there just to see what would happen. It simply could not have gotten there by itself.

At first, I decided to leave the kitten in the park. There were a lot of beautiful trees and bushes in the park. As I placed the kitten on a stone curb and examined it more carefully, I noticed the little kitten was a boy. He was dirty and smelling like kerosene, which did not prevent him from being very gentle.

After walking away from him, he began to follow me. Realizing that eventually he would end up on the roadway again and get run over by a car, I picked him up.

Now what? At home, I already had a cat that obviously would not want to have a new roommate.

Having only an hour to spare, I decided to take the foundling to my aunt, who lived nearby, and ask if I could keep him there until the evening. On the way over to her house, I bought him some milk.

My aunt made a sour face when she heard my idea, but agreed to shelter the kitten only until the evening. Because she believed her own Angora cat might pick a fight with the new kitten, she locked him in a separate room with a bowl of the milk I had bought and told me to return for him immediately after work.

Relieved and thankful to my aunt, I went back to work. I had missed my hair appointment and knew I would have to make another soon.

The rest of the day, I continued to think about the kitten. I couldn't put him back on the street, nor would my aunt keep him. So, I finally decided to keep him. Of course, my cat Aga would not be very happy, but eventually they would get used to each other and become friends, I thought.

It was settled. I got off work at 6 o'clock and went to my aunt's.

I picked up the kitten and came home. Since he was all dirty, I decided to bathe him first. I grabbed a towel and an insecticide pet shampoo, and took him into the bathroom.

I held the kitten with one hand and turned on the hot water, testing it with the other hand. I applied some shampoo on the kitten's back and tummy, lathered him, and started to rinse his little body.

The water was dark brown after the first washing and clearer after the second. However, it took a third washing to get the kitten clean. He had a great time and did not mind being turned and tickled all over. The shampoo washed off a lot of parasites. I dried the kitten with a blow-dryer and rubbed the inside of his ears with olive oil.

Now, sitting in front of me on my bed was a charming, black kitten with turquoise eyes. He was so cute, and at the same time quite pathetic, that it immediately inspired me to name him "Charm". After all, it seemed almost magical that we had found each other.

From that point on, Charm spent most of his time sleeping on my bed where he felt safest. I fed him every morning before going to work and placed him on the bedspread where he slept until I came home.

Aside from regular cat food, Charm really loved egg yolk. He was a very smart, serious, quiet, and calm cat.

CHAPTER 2

A year and a half later, Charm, who used to be an ordinary, small, short-haired street kitten, had become a splendid black panther with smooth, shiny fur and a piercing look in his green eyes (they gradually changed their color from turquoise to green).

He was a real handsome creature. His whole look, behavioral patterns, and even his gait emphasized his noble beauty.

I never saw him romping about like a silly little kitten. My other cat, Aga, was already two and a half years old, and he still did.

Aga was a beautiful ginger male cat with green eyes. He was a very playful and curious cat. He was used to getting a lot of attention as our only cat.

Aga didn't like Charm from the beginning. As a little cute kitten, Charm naturally needed more attention and care. Aga could feel it, despite of a lot of love, attention and care he got. It made him jealous. He hissed at Charm and even picked a fight with him sometimes.

But gradually, Charm got along with Aga and they became friends. They even began to sleep in one basket curled up together.

Charm was always well-behaved, clever, and self-assured. His confidence was striking.

Charm possessed a very strong aura. In the morning, he would come to wake me up. Lying in my bed, even with my eyes shut, I could feel his presence. It felt like a small bundle of heavenly energy which could not be mistaken for anything else. He was undoubtedly a very special cat.

I remember lying once with a hood over my face. I opened my eyes just a little as Charm approached me, straining his neck to see if I were still asleep under my hood.

Charm loved sleeping and lying on his back, stretching his body and spreading his limbs apart. He loved being patted on his tummy through thick, long fur.

On his back and belly, Charm had isolated strands of white fur. They were only visible if examined closely, with five or six patches overall.

The only thing I did not appreciate was the fact that Charm liked going outside.

We lived on the first floor, and in the summer our windows were constantly open. My bedroom window faced a small, unfenced garden and an old tall tree near it.

My father loved gardening and he planted a lot of different flowers and plants there. He liked to spend his spare time looking after his little garden and watering the plants. He even had three small lemon trees and saffron flowers growing there. There were a lot of weeds too and I helped to pull them out sometimes.

Farther down was a road and a railway, and behind them was an abandoned factory enclosed in a fence. There were fir trees growing near the fence. Usually, Charm went out into the garden for a little while and came back later.

One night, I noticed that he was crossing the road and climbing over the fence of the factory. Thank goodness it was quite late and there were no cars driving past, but who could assure me that he would not want to do it again some other time? How could I prevent him from doing that?

It was after that I started worrying about Charm. Something was constantly drawing him to the factory; I thought perhaps it was a female cat. I tried not to let him out, but to no avail. He always wanted to go outside.

A couple of times, Charm came back carrying birds. I think they were Hazel grouses, and he did not eat them. Later I found out that someone at the factory kept birds. Naturally, the bird owners probably did not like this at all.

At the end of the summer, my parents decided to refurbish our house and replace the old window frames that we had inherited from the previous owners. In order to escape the need to move out, we decided to replace the windows in one room at a time.

Charm sat on the floor, looking at me. "Shall I give you a bath, Charm?",

I asked and immediately realized there was no point in doing that before the restoration work ended.

In the morning, two contract workers came to change the window frames. I did not like either of them from the beginning. They talked a lot to each other. When they started taking down the old frames, both of my cats got frightened and ran out.

One of them came back after a couple of hours, but Charm was still gone. At first, I waited for him to show up, but he did not. With a heavy heart, I went out on the street looking for him.

CHAPTER 3

I missed Charm. I felt the need to take him in my arms and give him a hug. I kept looking at the photographs I had taken when he was a clumsy little kitten. Where is my Charm?

For several days in a row, I walked around the neighborhood calling his name. Alive or dead, he was nowhere to be seen. I realized he must have gotten in trouble and could not come back by himself. I was very upset and worried. I felt like he was somewhere calling for me.

On the evening of the thirteenth day, I was beginning to give up hope that I would find my Charm alive. I put on a sports suit, went out, and decided to follow my nose.

My instinct led me across the road, to the factory that overlooked our house. I had never been to the factory before. It was the end of the work day, so the place was quiet and dark, making it feel even more dangerous than before. Earlier that week, I had asked my brother to look around the grounds. I believed him when he said he had gone and that Charm was not there, however, I needed to look there myself.

I entered the factory court and started casting quick glances around. To my left, in front of the administrative building, several people stood around a car. On my right was a fence. Everywhere seemed clear; there was nothing more to see. Suddenly, fifty meters away from me, by the fence, I spotted something black lying on the asphalt. I quivered and quickly walked over there. I had found the dead body of a black animal.

The body had already decomposed, and there was nothing

left except black fur and long white bones showing through what was left of the fur. The rear legs were stretched out, revealing no flesh on them. The head was thrown back, and the mouth was open baring solid sharp fangs. One paw was broken and twisted. The shoulder blade was also crumpled and crushed by something heavy, and so were the cervical vertebrae. Strangely enough, the paws themselves were intact and had not decomposed. It was definitely the body of a cat.

No, this was not Charm, I told myself, as I bent towards the remains and examined them. This must have been some other black cat. Were Charm's rear legs that long?

I took out my mobile phone where I had Charm's photographs.

Comparing them to the remains, I tried to convince myself that this was not Charm. *The fangs looked similar, but fangs are common to all cats,* I told myself. No, this was not Charm.

I turned and began to walk away. I only managed to walk a few steps, but couldn't leave and went back.

The fact that there were no other black cats in the neighborhood, and that Charm had been gone for thirteen days, started to convince me that these were indeed Charm's remains.

Bending over them, I could discern Charm's scent through the smell of decay.

And then I noticed the white strands on the black fur, just like Charm used to have, and I was left with no doubt. I began to cry.

CHAPTER 4

I cannot recall how much time I spent bending over my Charm, breathing in his smell, and crying quietly.

At that moment, I was very angry and, in a heartbeat, I would have taken my anger out on the person who did this.

I got up, rubbed my tears away, and looked around. The car was still nearby, along with the group of people, possibly workers, next to it. I approached them and asked who had run over that cat. Each of them declared they had not done it.

One of them introduced himself as the court custodian and said that the cat had not been run over but had eaten poison. He pointed to a spot about twenty meters away from the place Charm had been lying, where according to him, Charm had vomited blood after he had been poisoned. Then somehow Charm found the strength to move elsewhere (not where he was now) and had died there (having broken a limb and his neck). I understood perfectly that they were lying to me.

It was getting late. I was devastated and felt very tired. I had to think about burying my cat, but I needed my dad's help. I returned home, and after listening to my story, Dad said it would be best to do it in the next morning. He assured me that nothing would happen to the remains overnight. I didn't want to leave Charm; he had already been there for too long. But I agreed that burying him in the morning was indeed a better idea.

Naturally, that night I did not get any sleep. I occasionally approached the window, staring toward the spot where Charm's body was. It was exactly opposite my bedroom window, across the road, on the other side of the factory fence.

CHAPTER 5

Drizzling rain started that night and went on all morning.

Just after sunrise, I grabbed an old dress to wrap Charm in, and Dad and I went to pick him up.

As we walked, I wept. My dad told me about a tricolored cat he had as a child and how heavy boxes had crushed it. He told me how much it upset him. Although he was trying to comfort me, it was not making me feel better.

When we reached that cursed place, I noticed the rain had made the body decompose much faster, revealing all the bones.

I stood in the rain, crying and gazing on what was left of Charm. I thought about how I had planned to bathe him just before he ran away and how the rain had, in a way, done that for me. I blamed myself—I was a

Leyla Atke

bad pet owner. Perhaps, if I had bathed him, everything would have worked out differently.

Still crying, I carefully placed the remains on my old dress, wrapping and taking them in my arms. Then Dad and I went to bury Charm.

After a short discussion, we decided to bury him by my bedroom window, under the old tree. Thick, tall grass grew there in the summer. Charm loved sitting on the windowsill and watching the scenery. How ironic.

Dad brought a shovel and started digging. Although the earth was soft, he hit a root, and it became more difficult to dig.

Soon, Dad dug out a hole and told me to put Charm in it, but the hole did not seem deep enough to me, so I asked him to dig more.

When everything was finally ready, I laid my Charm in there and stood still. I had failed to protect him. I had a strong desire to do something special for him. I had an idea.

I ran inside the house and came out with an egg and Charm's bowl. I cracked the egg, put it in the bowl, and set it at the head of the grave. Charm loved eggs very much.

I shed a flood of tears as I used my hand to fill the grave with dirt. Soon I had another very strange idea. I remembered reading how some tribes sacrificed animals to their dead, so they would have something to eat in the afterlife. I thought about sacrificing a rooster at the grave as soon as possible. I knew it was wrong, but I was intuitively trying to find a balance. I cannot explain this from logical point of view and I would never even think about this in my normal condition. The shock of Charm's loss had caused me to temporarily lose my ability to think clearly. Immediately, I shared my idea with Dad. Seeing the state I was in, he agreed straight away. This calmed me down a bit.

However, the next day, having consulted with Mom and his friends, Dad told me that this would count as a sacrifice to an animal, which was contrary to all religions, and everyone began trying to talk me out of the idea.

My uncle said that no one knew what would come out of an animal sacrifice and that it might even be dangerous. He said I might experience bad karma, and it was most likely illegal.

For a moment, I could understand primitive humans who supplied their dead with everything they might have needed in their afterlife, including pots, clothing, animals, and even their wives.

Yes, I wanted to send Charm a rooster, but could not sacrifice one myself. Actually, it saddens me to hear of animals being killed, even when it is done for subsistence purposes. I am against it. But at that moment, I was not thinking straight.

I did not end up finding anyone who could do this for me. Yet, for a while, a strong desire lingered in my mind, and I thought I was simply going mad. I wanted to do something really big for Charm, but what could I do? I had decided it would not be right to take another animal's life as a gift to Charm, but was still very hurt. I was lost and frustrated. I tried to figure out what to do in order to comfort myself. But I couldn't do anything to change the situation.

I would never find out what really happened to Charm. Had he been run over by a car? Or had he really been poisoned and then run over by a car?

Or had street dogs torn him to pieces? Only God knows.

Another unpleasant fact in this story was linked to my brother.

Remember how I had asked him to go to the factory and look for Charm? Well, he did go, but later confessed he had lied to me. He had seen a dead cat that day, but didn't tell me, figuring it wasn't Charm. And the intestines that were sticking out of the body had scared him. But he could have mentioned this to me. He could have simply told me, "Leyla, there is something suspicious in the factory yard. Go check it out." Was it really that difficult and was it necessary to lie?

Then I realized that Charm's death had occurred on September 30, my brother's birthday. He probably didn't want to deal with a dead cat on that day. I did not want to think that he did it on purpose.

And one thing was true—I had been lucky enough to have discovered Charm even after he'd been missing for thirteen days, and had still been able to give him a proper burial.

CHAPTER 6

One evening, I stuffed myself with different fruits. I do not remember what they were; I just remember mixing things I had never mixed before. This always makes me have vivid dreams.

I found that same insecticide pet shampoo with the scent of meadow plants that I once used to bathe Charm. I breathed in its smell and remembered Charm. Before going to bed, I began looking through Charm's photos.

That night, I had a dream about walking through a beautiful fairytale forest with fanciful trees. It felt very realistic. After walking through a curtain of swarming butterflies, I noticed my Charm sitting on a bough stretching close to the forest floor. I rejoiced and began calling him: "Charm! Charm!" but he did not hear me. Charm kept looking somewhere to the side. What a beauty he was! Yes, this was my Charm! At this point, a sunray shone on him gracefully through the tree branches. I approached him and noticed that his eyes were pink.

As I woke up, still half asleep and lying with my eyes shut, I felt Charm's presence near me, very close, somewhere to the left, around ten centimeters away from my head. This was his Bundle of Energy! I could not confuse it with anything else.

Now fully awake but afraid to move, for fear I would scare the spirit away, I lay happily and enjoyed its presence. It felt as if I was in paradise. Charm was near! Many times, when he was alive, I could feel his aura this strongly in his presence. Even with my eyes closed.

I felt much better. Besides, time had passed and my life was marked with many new events. It had been a year since I lost Charm.

CHAPTER 7

September 30, 2008. Early morning. Meowing outside my bedroom window woke me up. I ran to my window and opened it. What did I see? Just a couple of steps away from Charm's grave, there was a little black kitten!

The kitten looked very vulnerable and desperate. It was all alone on the street, his mother was missing.

There were no cars on the road in front of my house.

For a few minutes, I stood still and tried to comprehend what I was seeing. I decided to pick up the kitten immediately. I tried to bend over the window in order to see if I could grab it. But I couldn't reach the kitten from my window. It was too high.

As soon as the kitten noticed me, it started meowing louder and came really close to the wall under my window. It placed its paws against the wall, trying to climb up.

Suddenly, I heard my mother's voice telling me that there was a little black kitten outside, about to be attacked by street dogs. The little black kitten woke her up too, and she was very concerned about the situation.

I couldn't see street dogs from my bedroom window. But my mother's bedroom was on the other side of the house with a different view.

She came to me in my room already all dressed up and with her outdoor shoes on. Mom looked very concerned. It looked like she was ready to go out and pick up the kitten.

"Then what are you waiting for?! Go get it quickly!", I shouted. To be honest, I did this so that, in the future, I would not get blamed for picking up another cat from the street.

Mom went outside to get the kitten while I kept watch out the window to make sure it was not harmed. A couple of minutes later, I held the little one in my hands. It was a boy. He had a very little fur; in some areas it barely covered the skin. He was very young, hardly a month old. On his chest, he had white strands on the black fur, just like my Charm had. That similarity particularly surprised me.

I do not know how the little black kitten ended up on the street all alone, without his mother.

Apparently, the kitten lost his mother and somehow appeared near Charm's grave, under my bedroom window.

It was a very special moment for both of us. We both needed each other so much.

I felt as if I had discovered a treasure. I carefully examined the kitten to see if it was harmed. Luckily, everything was okay and I decided to bathe the kitten first. It was a good idea. The water washed off dirt and parasites. The little black kitten didn't mind being bathed and actually enjoyed it very much.

In ten minutes, the kitten was already bathed and groomed, sitting on my bed in my bedroom. I went in the kitchen to get an olive oil and rubbed the inside of his ears with it.

The little black kitten looked calm and comfortable. I was very touched. We looked happily at each other, and from that moment on, I understood that we needed each other; and we belong to each other to the rest of our lives.

I thanked God for being so forgiving and returning my delightful Charm back to me.

Naturally, there would be no more wandering the streets for Charm from now on, vaccinations and neutering are a must.

Charm's favorite spot is my bed. He can spend half of the day sleeping on it all curled up. Every morning, Charm jumps on my bed and curls around my neck like a collar. He begins purring like a steam engine while biting my lower lip and pulling it towards him. Sometimes Charm bites me on the nose.

Charm is full of life, impulsive, curious, and aggressive. When Charm is overwhelmed with emotions, he starts talking—in his own language, of course. He meows loudly, impulsively and continuously, as if trying to say something. Such emotions can be evoked, for example, by a piece of wallpaper hanging down by the ceiling. Charm feels obliged to pull it off completely. For that, he jumps on the door. He will not rest until he reaches his goal.

When I am working and too focused on a document to notice him, Charm climbs on my desk and lies on the project. His intention is to distract me from my work and completely draw all my attention to him. He loves playing with his own tail, trying to grab it and spinning like a whirligig. Charm adores egg yolk and mussels.

And, to me, he still remains a little mystery.

About the Author

Leyla Atke is a mother and an award-winning author. She lives in Denmark. Since her childhood, she loved reading. Her influences are Alexandre Dumas, Maurice Druon, Victor Hugo, H. G. Wells, and Leo Tolstoy.

Leyla Atke has been featured on Bestsellersworld.com, Fiction Frenzy TV, Red River Radio and some others.

Her book "Charm: An Amazing Story of a Little Black Cat" was honored as a Finalist in Children's Non-Fiction category of 2012 International Book Awards and as a Finalist in Non-Fiction Animals category of 2012 Readers Favorite Book Award Contest.

It won 2014 Readers Favorite Honorable Mention in Non-Fiction Short Story category and 2015

Readers Favorite Honorable Mention in Non-Fiction Animals category.

Leyla's hobbies include archaeology, paleontology, history, tennis & fitness.

Ms. Atke is in the process of writing her second book about Charm.

Find out more about Leyla Atke on her author website: www.leylaatke.com

www.ingramcontent.com/pod-product-compliance
Lightning Source LLC
LaVergne TN
LVHW010028070426
835513LV00001B/13